RAISING RESPONSIBLE ADULTS

What Every Intentional Parent Needs to Know

Dr. Randy Carlson

Raising Responsible Adults—What Every Intentional
Parent Needs to Know

Published by Family Life Communications Incorporated

PO Box 35300
Tucson, AZ 85704

TheIntentionalLife.com

ACKNOWLEDGEMENTS

I need to congratulate my team for the excellent job they have done by including in this study guide many of the biblical principles I teach in my national radio program, *Intentional Living,* and the teachings of several respected educators.

Editing *Donna Carlson, Dawn Heitger and Shanna Gregor*
Layout & Design *Jimmy Anaya*

Several of the parenting concepts in this study guide originated from the works of Drs. Alfred Alder and Rudolph Dreikurs.

FOREWORD

Randy & Donna Carlson

Donna and I had been married for a couple of years when we decided that the time was right for us to have a family. Like most young couples we thought that in only a matter of weeks we would be announcing to the world that another Carlson was on the way – but God had another plan for us. Apparently God wasn't impressed with our self-reliance.

The following years were filled with pain and frustration – we were infertile and there was nothing we could do about it. Eventually, we came face-to-face with the prognosis we feared the most: "It's not likely that you two will ever conceive and have children of your own." It wasn't the kind of news we had hoped for or, frankly, were ready to accept.

Then, adding insult to injury, our well-meaning but communicationally-challenged doctor went on to say in half question and half statement form, "Why would you want to bring children into this world anyway?" While his weak attempt at comfort was not at all helpful, his message was clear – parenting isn't all it's cracked up to be…so forget it and get on with your life!

Donna and I were not about to take this pronouncement as final. We naively assumed anything could be fixed– including our infertility. So we spent the next several years jumping from doctor to doctor looking for someone who could help make things better for us. Nothing changed much except our frustration and discouragement.

It wasn't until we finally committed all of our hurt, loss and frustration to Christ, willingly accepted His apparent plan for our lives, and turned our efforts and emotions toward the long adoption process that the news came –

Donna was pregnant! We were excited, fearful and ill equipped for parenting. We had spent a great deal more time thinking about getting a child than on how to raise one. Like most young parents we had dreams for our children but little preparation. These were exciting, nail-biting days in our young lives.

Over the years God continued to bless and today we have three grown children, two daughters-in-law, a son-in-law and two beautiful grandchildren. It was a joy to watch our children grow and develop into uniquely different human beings with their own lives and interests. But there were also times when it was baffling to know how to respond appropriately and intentionally to each individual personality.

My desire for you as you turn the pages of this book is that its principles will help you to avoid some of the mistakes that are all too common in parenting. The following pages will give you a blueprint to work from in areas of discipline and correction.

We've learned that parenting is a big deal and requires intentional parents to pull it off. It's the biggest job couples will ever have in life, and the fact you are about to jump into this parenting resource is confirmation of your desire to do this job right.

I pray that God will use the content to encourage you in the process of intentionally raising your children to become the responsible adults He created them to be.

Dr. Randy L. Carlson

Dr. Randy Carlson,
President, Family Life Communications Incorporated
Host, *Intentional Living*

CONTENTS

Introduction

Most of us enter parenthood with wide-eyed wonder, our heads full of vague hopes and still-to-be-molded dreams for our child.

We're in awe over the gift of life that has been entrusted to us. So even before we trace its infant form on the ultrasound screen or sign those adoption papers, we look joyfully ahead and begin making plans for this child's future. We want him or her to be healthy and happy, of course. Beyond that, we usually declare ourselves content.

Then as that child's personality takes shape and his or her life unfolds in our presence, our naiveté starts to crumble even while our dreams for this life entrusted to us take firmer shape and grow more sophisticated. We still yearn for healthy, yes. And happy would be good, too. We continue to be in awe of this gift of life, but as the challenges of parenting confront us, we realize we want more than just healthy and happy – significantly more. We want *responsibility*. We want to raise a child who will contribute something positive to this world.

Somewhere along this life's way – perhaps it was the first time your toddler conked another child over the head with a plastic toy – you realized that hopes for good health might just have been the easiest dream of all. For the most part, health is in God's hands. And happiness – you can pave the way but the choice tends to rest with your child. But as you took the toy weapon away from your child and tried to explain why we don't smack others when we're frustrated, maybe you finally came face to face with the daunting realization that the responsibility part has a whole lot to do with you. And as the years creep by, and you encounter messy rooms or less than stellar report cards, defiance and an ongoing bad attitude, that realization will likely hit – hard – over and over again. You want *responsibility* in your child. In fact, the whole world needs it! It takes understanding, planning and some good old-fashioned hard work – on your part as much as your child's.

So hang on to those dreams. You can be an effective parent, and your child can become a functioning, contributing member of society. Some wisdom – mixed with a whole lot of prayer – practically and consistently applied will go a long way in raising a responsible adult as you choose to parent intentionally.

This book will help you identify keys to effective parenting and discover new ways to apply them. Then as you seek the Lord and ask for His blessings on your child, you may find yourself molding a life of which every parent dreams.

CHAPTER 1

God Has a Vision for Your Child

Margo attended a parenting workshop where she was asked to complete an exercise designed to help her gain insight into the great adventure she'd started called parenting. The assignment was to find the one perfect word that would communicate the essence of parenting.

All the parents in the room hunched over their papers, brows furrowed, trying to come up with that one key description. Margo watched with interest as one by one the other parents held up their words. They'd come up with some great words, ones full of hope and promise – like *awesome* and *fulfilling*. There were some other, more tentative words, like challenging and risky. But Margo's word got the biggest laugh – and was quickly recognized by the group facilitator as probably the most honest. Margo was quite certain that hers was probably the most heartfelt. Margo's one-word communication on parenting: *HELP!!!*

No matter where you are on the parenting curve – prenatal, infancy, toddlerhood, childhood or in the adolescent stage of child rearing – chances are you've already found yourself in the vise of panic as you grappled with the reality that children arrive without instruction manuals.

At some point we must acknowledge that when it comes to raising our children, we're forced to rely solely on good counsel, inner wisdom and our own instincts. Although the advice and examples of others can aid and comfort us, we can't depend on someone else to tell us what to do in every situation – primarily because there's no guarantee that our child will respond exactly like another. So what's a parent to do? Where do we go for insight and understanding?

Contrary to what many people think, wisdom is neither a byproduct of intelligence nor something we're either born with or without. Instead, like harvesting a crop, wisdom is something that we gather in throughout our lives, through knowledge and accumulated experiences – ours or someone else's – especially those that we try to view through a prism of understanding.

Psalm 111:10 tells us *The fear of the Lord is the beginning of wisdom.* Effective parenting starts with respect for God. In parenting we must be prepared to defer our desires and wishes for our child to God's. We also must be prepared to help our child view life through this prism, too. Because every child is an individual and unique creation, God has a plan and a purpose for each of us that is both the same yet different from any other created beings. Helping your child discover and conform to God's vision for him or her is the highest and most sacred calling of parenting.

> Make no mistake, God wants you to be the best parent you can be

A Higher Purpose

You're probably reading this book because you've already come to the realization that you want more for your child

than a simple vision of health and happiness. Even if you
have no expectations of raising a child prodigy or a future
president – although you just might be – you still want
your child to reach his or her maximum potential. Rest
assured that every child, no matter how rough the edges,
has potential.

Ephesians 2:10 declares, *For we are God's workmanship,
created in Christ Jesus to do good works, which God prepared
in advance for us to do.* Make no mistake; if you are a parent, God wants you to be the best parent you can be. But
parenting isn't always easy, and helping your child reach his
or her full potential won't always be a breeze either. Most of
us need help as parents. Fortunately, our greatest resource
remains readily available.

If we want to fulfill the vision that God has for us as parents,
or our children, we must get to know Jesus Christ.

A Model Child

We get a glimpse of what a life lived according to God's
vision looks like through the person of Jesus. And Jesus
grew in wisdom and stature, and in favor with God and
men (Luke 2:52). Long before He was identified as the
Savior of the world, everyone who knew Him held Jesus
in high esteem. The Scriptures don't give us many details
about Jesus' lifestyle as a youngster, but we know that good
reputations are not bestowed by chance or coincidence, but
earned. Proverbs 20:11 tells us, *Even a child is known by his
actions, by whether his conduct is pure and right.* Most of
us think of *stature* as meaning physical height. But *stature*
also refers to esteem. From boyhood on Jesus undoubtedly
practiced a righteousness that was plain for all to see and
commanded respect.

The Bible is a vivid testimony of the life of Jesus. God wants all His children – both young and old – to steadily grow in knowledge of Jesus until we begin to resemble Him in our thoughts, words and actions. To continue to grow more like Jesus we must pursue lifelong habits of Bible study and prayer.

A Child's – But Not Childish – Responsibility

The underlying principle that shaped Jesus' life as a boy probably comes as no new revelation. God has been so direct about His expectations of children that very few of us can plead ignorance. Although many of the Ten Commandments apply to people of all ages, God directly addressed children through one.

Exodus 20:12 says, *Honor your father and your mother, so that you may live long in the land the Lord your God is giving you.* Like many proverbs and promises of God, this Scripture should not be interpreted to mean that every child who lives a good, obedient life is guaranteed to reach old age. Certainly many obedient, godly children have had their lives cut short through no fault of their own while some of the most disobedient and unruly people on earth have lived life to ripe old ages.

But this Scripture should remind us that parents entrusted with children are to protect and nurture them. When children are obedient to parents who take that charge seriously, they will likely prolong their lives as they avoid the dangers and snares of this world. For example, how many children's lives have been prolonged simply because they listened when their parents told them to look both ways before crossing the street?

Maybe you remember a time in your own childhood or adolescence when you ignored your own desires to heed your parents' advice or instructions and were spared problems or difficulties of your own making.

The Apostle Paul reiterated God's command: *Children, obey your parents in the Lord, for this is right. "Honor your father and mother"* – *which is the first commandment with a promise* – *"that it may go well with you and that you may enjoy long life on the earth"* (Ephesians 6:1-3).

Paul clarifies a parental responsibility that goes along with this command and promise. Read Ephesians 6:4, *Fathers, do not exasperate your children; instead bring them up in the training and instruction of the Lord.*

In Philippians 2:5 and 8 the Apostle Paul once again held up Jesus as a role model: *Your attitude should be the same as that of Jesus Christ ... he humbled himself and became obedient to death – even death on a cross!* Underline the word obedient in Philippians 2:8. At what age do you suppose obedience becomes unimportant in life?

If you said *never* you would be right! As followers of Christ we should always be ready to submit to God. But if we never learn biblical submission, society will still demand its own kind. Each of us has authorities in our lives – governments and employers – to whom we are accountable.

When you train your child to obey, you are giving him or her an understanding to know and please Christ

The most important reason to teach our children obedience is because we want them to please God, but there is also a good practical reason for children to obey their parents. Learning obedience to their parents teaches children how to be accepted and productive in society. It also sets the stage for their own strong relationship with Christ.

An intentional life in Christ is following the instruction found in Ephesians 5:10, *Figure out what will please Christ, and then do it* (MSG). When you train your child to obey, you are giving him or her an understanding that they will use for the rest of their life in their journey to know and please Christ. You're giving them what they need to reach their maximum potential.

The Parent's Responsibility

To raise a responsible adult you must know and obey God's precepts, or laws, yourself. In other words, to raise responsible children you must be a responsible parent! Then you must teach your child to be the same. Read Proverbs 22:6, *Train a child in the way he should go, and when he is old he will not turn from it.* According to this, the primary duty of a parent is to train a child in God's precepts. The conditional promise attached to this verse is that when he or she is older, they will continue to follow in the Lord's ways.

We'll look more closely at that promise from God, but first, let's examine the task of training children. What do you think child training encompasses? Check all that apply.

❏ Potty training   ❏ Work Ethics

❏ Bible study   ❏ Virtues

❏ Manners   ❏ Telling time

❏ Tying shoes   ❏ Managing finances

❏ Reading and writing   ❏ Healthy eating habits

❏ How to get along with others   ❏ Decision-making skills

Did you check off everything? The parental job is expansive and varied, seemingly endless—and the above checklist is only a limited sample of an unlimited task list. Look at the tasks again. Put a star beside the achievements that may not be accomplished without a parent's involvement.

If looking at just a sample of the parenting task that lies ahead for you seems overwhelming, you'll be pleased to know that there is a secret to parenting. The vital task for you as a parent

The parent has been given the responsibility for what a child knows and understands about God

is to teach your child about God, who will instruct your child Himself and fill in any gaps you leave in the process. Deuteronomy 6:6-9 provides a plan.

These commandments that I give you today are to be upon your hearts. Impress them on your children. Talk about them when you sit at home and when you walk along the road, when you lie down and when you get up. Tie them as symbols on your hands and bind them on your foreheads. Write them on the doorframes of your houses and on your gates.

From reading this, you can see that parents have the responsibility for teaching children about the goodness of God. Our talk should revolve around God, our minds should be constantly fixed on Him and our actions should reflect that devotion. We are to fill our hearts, our homes and our hours with Him in such a way that our children cannot help but notice – and perhaps emulate.

Although our churches are great support in this endeavor, it is the parent who has been given the responsibility for what a child knows and understands about God.

The Apostle Paul gave a good description of the labor-intensive enterprise of teaching others about Christ in Galatians 5:19, *My dear children, for whom I am again in the pains of childbirth until Christ is formed in you...* Paul compared training others to be a disciple of Jesus to the physical task of childbirth.

Let's draw some analogies. If physical childbirth begins in the womb, then spiritual birth begins in the heart. Likewise if physical childbirth takes some time, we can't expect spiritual training to be a quick enterprise. We know that children often have growth spurts. If you think about it, the first year is an astonishing time of growth. We could naturally assume that someone might be especially prone to a spiritual growth spurt the first year they receive salvation. Considering the longevity of the spiritual growth process, do you feel you have devoted adequate time to teaching your child about God?

I believe these are the key precepts we should be teaching our children. Aside from honoring one's parents, consider the following verses to determine some of the virtues that God wants you to impress on your children as they mature.

> Hebrews 5:14: To learn the difference between good and evil.
>
> Hebrews 8:10: To put God's laws in their minds and hearts.
>
> Proverbs 13:20: To choose good friends.
>
> Ephesians 5:3: To keep themselves sexually pure.

Obviously, the commands of God extend far beyond this. But if you can impress these values on your children, you will be preparing them well for adulthood.

Let's go back to Proverbs 22:6. Most of us know families whose children caused their parents lots of heartbreak through rebellion. You might have even heard those parents lament: "We taught him better than this." So does Proverbs 22:6 promise what it says or not?

Like other proverbs, this one is best considered a rule of thumb. Parents who are intentional about training their children usually end up with responsible adults—although sometimes that responsibility was hard learned through dealing with the repercussions of a period of rebellion. That's where the "old" often comes in. But like Adam and Eve, some of us will find ourselves with children who go their own disobedient way. While training our children is not an iron-clad guarantee that they'll turn out well, it's perfectly true that, given enough time, our aging children often will come to the realization that God's ways are always best.

> God can go with our children where we as parents cannot

The Great Rewards

Although most of us as parents hope that our children will always be willing to listen to our counsel, we also know that we won't always be in a position to give it. It's a great comfort, therefore, to know that God can go with our children where we as parents cannot. Isaiah 54:13 says, *All your sons will be taught by the Lord, and great will be your children's peace.* When God becomes your child's personal teacher and mentor peace is the result. In our dreams of happiness for our children, isn't this what we really seek for them? We know that life can be tough, even for Christians. God didn't promise to insulate any of us from the troubles of this world. No matter how dedicated and diligent we are as parents, we cannot provide environments for our children that are devoid of conflict or trouble-free.

But we can lead our children to an incredible inner resource that will sustain them during tough times. *Yet to all who received him, to those who believed in his name, he gave the right to become children of God* (John 1:12). When your child is ready to make a decision to accept Christ, it's important that you are ready to guide him through the process. Romans 10:9 says, *That if you confess with your mouth, "Jesus is Lord," and believe in your heart that God raised him from the dead, you will be saved.*

The Next Right ONE THING

If you haven't already, establish a practice of family devotions. Yours can be as unique as your family, designed to fit the ages, interests and activities of your children. The point is to set aside time for family worship and prayer. It can be a time for each family member to share what he or she is thankful for. You can sing praise songs together or read a Bible story. Make it respectful but fun. Don't try to make it too long; God

If you give a child generations of faith as his background, you give him the ultimate head start in life

wants our time with Him to be relaxed and joyful. Determine that this week – even if you don't plan to make it a habit – your family will have a special time of devotions. If you already do family devotions, this week maybe you can focus on how God is the perfect Father.

Generation Why?

It's really not a mystery why some kids seem to have a natural affinity for the gospel. They are born to it! Two books of the New Testament were written to Timothy, apparently one of the Apostle Paul's favored sons in the faith.

In 2 Timothy 1:5, Paul clues us in on why Timothy was such a promising protégé of Christianity. His mother Eunice and his grandmother Lois trained him in the way to go. Timothy's faith was nourished from childhood on. God can take any person at any point in his life and redeem him, but if you give a child generations of faith as his background, you give him the ultimate head start in life.

CHAPTER 2

How to Understand Your Child

Having resigned yourself to the idea that children don't come with instruction manuals, you'll need to prepare to unlock the mysteries of *your* child's identity yourself. Decide to become the expert on your child. Other people may be able to supply you with pieces of the puzzle during his lifetime – teachers will provide insight on his behavior at school, for example – but they are more likely to rely on your knowledge to help them understand your child than the other way around.

Fortunately, learning about your child can be the most exciting discovery you'll ever make. That awe and reverence of life will return to you over and over as you discover some new ability or unique characteristic. But make no mistake about it; the delicate task of exploring your child's inner self takes time and finesse. Don't settle for a quick analysis and then pigeonhole your child accordingly. Just as soon as you congratulate yourself on having your little darling all figured out, you'll be greeted by a stranger who looks and sounds a lot like your child but acts completely different (especially during adolescence). That's the beauty (and irony) of child rearing; as a child grows, you'll keep on finding new facets to his personality to explore.

Psalm 139:13-14 reminds us of just how intricate a human being truly is. *For you created my inmost being; you knit me together in my mother's womb. I praise you because I am fearfully and wonderfully made.*

The psalmist is clearly marveling at God's handiwork, but what do you suppose he meant when he referred to his inmost being? How would you define your inmost being?

The psalmist was referring not to internal organs but the emotional center of a person. Psalm 139:1-4 hints at just what comprises our inmost being.

> *O Lord, you have searched me and you know me. You know when I sit and when I rise; you perceive my thoughts from afar. You discern my going out and my lying down; you are familiar with all my ways. Before a word is on my tongue you know it completely, O LORD.* Psalm 139:1-4

Our inmost being isn't just a collection of blood and tissue, bone and muscles. Our inmost being refers to our mental processes and sensitivities and how they work together to shape our behavior and influence our decision-making. Obviously, we can't emulate God the Father in His omniscient ability to discern everything there is to know about a person. But as parents we can strive to be attuned to our child as much as possible.

Think about your spouse or another family member you know very well. Suppose you wrecked their car and called to explain what happened and to apologize. Do you know what that person would say in return? After many years of marriage or living with someone, if we pay attention, we know him or her well enough to know what he or she will say before the words come from his or her mouth. That's exactly the way God the Father knows each of His children.

It's the kind of relationship you want to develop with your own offspring; keeping in mind that God has created our inner beings with as much complexity as our physical bodies. While we should never presume to know all there is to know about someone else, we can attempt to peel away the layers of the human spirit that lives within your child.

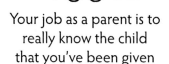

Your job as a parent is to really know the child that you've been given

One mother called *Intentional Living* to tell us how she's doing just that:

> *My daughter and I have entered the teen years. Rather than going into a mother's rant using too many words, I finally just said, "Lord what is the better way?" And his response was "fewer words." I've discovered I can say what I need to say and then be done, trusting the Holy Spirit will finish the job and have that conversation with my daughter.*

Temperament and Personality

Contrary to classical psychology that suggests that children arrive as blank slates whose personalities can be imprinted by their environments, you've probably already learned that your child was born with a distinct, unique and innate nature that belongs only to him or her. Some experts suggest that a child's basic personality isn't completely formed until about age 5 to 7, so your parenting will greatly influence his personality, especially in those early years. While experience has proven that children arrive in our homes and families already wired to their peculiar inner workings, your job as a parent is to really know the child that you've been given and help that child intentionally refine his personality to bring out the best characteristics possessed.

Family Atmosphere

How a family interacts as a unit also will have great influence on the development of a child's personality. Families that emphasize organization and sets of rules, for example, will likely produce children who highly value organization themselves and rely on regulations to help them know the boundaries in life. Families that place an emphasis on freedom of expression are more likely to have free-spirited children, who may have trouble setting or distinguishing boundaries without help.

Prevailing attitudes often stem from the family atmospheres present in homes where the parents were raised. For example, strict, repressive homes may produce children who grow up to be legalistic, overbearing parents. Children raised in that atmosphere, depending upon their individual makeup, will either likely rebel against it, or become overly cautious in adulthood themselves. Moreover, family crises and problems can have effects on a child. Parents who are tense and worried about finances may find themselves parenting a child overly interested in making money.

The home should provide an atmosphere of love and attention

While families, like individuals, take on unique personalities, there is one contributing factor that will help produce happy, well-rounded children: the home should provide an atmosphere of love and attention. This is one thing you should strive to be very intentional about.

Family Constellation

Just like with stars, the family constellation refers to the make-up of your family – where each individual fits in the grouping. Factors include parents or other adults in the home, the number of children in the home, and the birth order and gender of each child. Birth order and gender can often play a significant role in the development of each member's personality.

The Oldest Child

The oldest child in the family spends their first years of life surrounded by adults and having their parents all to themselves. These and other factors often influence the development traits of a perfectionist. Oldest children tend to set high standards for themselves and others and often feel a great sense of responsibility and a need to please others. These are the children most often described as "10 years old going on 30." Oldest children are often natural leaders, well organized and in many cases, academically oriented. The oldest child is often a high achiever and can be perceived by others as serious, controlling and bossy.

The Middle Child

Middle children can possess a unique combination of personality traits because of the influence of older and younger siblings. They typically get along with a wide variety of people, are less dependent upon family members, are good at negotiating and are often patient and tolerant of others. Middle children can also be competitive as a result of being sandwiched in between older and younger siblings, and having to share the family's resources. They also tend to be cooperative and very loyal. Knowing exactly where they best fit in the family can be a significant challenge for the middle child, so they may also spend much of their time outside of the family, which may result in being seen as the "problem" child.

The Youngest Child

It is not uncommon for the youngest child in the family to receive a great deal of attention from Mom and Dad as well as older brothers and sisters. Because of having older siblings, they are often given less responsibility, allowing them to focus more on playing and less on working.

By the time the last child is born Mom and Dad are often more experienced, relaxed and tired. They spend less time and energy in the parenting process than they did with their first child and consequently place fewer expectations and demands on their youngest. The "baby of the family" is often fun loving and easy going, tends not to take life too seriously and enjoys getting a lot of attention from others. The youngest child can be very friendly and develop great social skills, but they can also be manipulative and expect others to take care of them. The youngest child often struggles with feelings of inferiority when comparing themselves to older siblings.

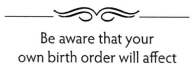

Be aware that your own birth order will affect how you parent

You also should be aware that your own birth order will affect how you parent. If you're a firstborn parenting a firstborn, that relationship may contain two highly performing perfectionists – so butting heads may be just a little more likely. On the other hand, if you were the lastborn in your family, you may have a tendency to focus on the fun side of parenting – a wonderful attribute unless you neglect more serious demands .

Keep in mind that your spouse also will bring his or her own place in the family to the equation. Some of the inevitable disagreements over childrearing that you as parents must work through together will likely be a result of the way you view life differently from the vantage of your family constellation.

If your children don't fit into the descriptions above, don't be concerned. As mentioned earlier, there are many factors that influence your child's personality development – birth order is only one of them. And even that can be impacted by variables, such as the fact that if there is a five-year space between one sibling and the next, the younger one is likely to respond to life more like a first-born.

Parental and Social Expectations

How you treat your child and the culture surrounding him will have its impact. Your own expectations for your child will undoubtedly affect his behavior. One of the principles of *Intentional Parenting* is to recognize that children will usually give you what you expect. In other words, the standards that you set are the ones your children will meet. Neglect to set standards, and you children won't know what you expect. Sometimes, it's that simple.

That said, it's also important to note that understanding the power of expectation means we also have to be careful that the ones we place on our children are realistic and, most importantly, match up to God's.

Let's use school as an example because most parents want their children to excel in scholastics. Here again you have to know your child. Did his problem-solving ability impress you from an early age? Is he or she a creative thinker? How artistic is your child? While we must always encourage them to do their best, we should not require or expect our children to be able to perform outside of their God-given abilities to meet our parental (and very human) expectations. Why expect your artistic child to be a math genius when God apparently wired him to be the former? Many children have been frustrated by parental expectations that don't match up with God's. Therefore, your expectations for your child must be defined by God's expectations. Again Ephesians 6:4 says *Fathers, do not exasperate your children; instead, bring them up in the training and instruction of the Lord.*

To parent wisely, we must have knowledge and understanding of the world he experiences every day

While we train our children, we should be paying attention to their bent and how they're wired. We are to lead them "in the way he should go." That way is God's way – with all their positive, innate traits and characteristics already leaning in that direction.

An important component to understanding your child, especially in adolescence, is to understand the culture he lives in. To parent wisely, we must have knowledge and understanding of the world he experiences every day.

When Jesus sent His disciples out to do His works, He understood what they would be facing, according to Matthew 10:16, *I am sending you out like sheep among wolves. Therefore, be as shrewd as snakes and as innocent as doves.*

Part of knowing your child is recognizing what he's up against on a daily basis. Sometimes, in their own best interests, we must work to remove temptations from our children's paths.

Knowing your child may be just a little more difficult than you think. Recognizing their favorite food as a baby is a lot easier than knowing whom your child sits with at lunch. It only takes a little research, but it's the kind of knowledge that can be overlooked – and the kind of information that can give you great insight to what's going on in your child's life. It takes time to know your child. Be sure to take the time!

A Parent Should Know These Things

When Jesse rounded up his sons to parade them in front of Samuel so the prophet could anoint the one God wanted to be king (1 Samuel 16:1-13), it didn't even occur to him to include his youngest, David. Instead he left David busily tending sheep while the rest of Jesse's brood, impressive in their own rights, took turns meeting Samuel.

But it was David, the one who would later slay a giant, the one who would be dubbed a man "after God's own heart," who was destined to be anointed. Had Jesse overlooked noble qualities of courage and faith in his young son or just the potential for them? With such a large family, it was probably all too easy to do – but imagine his disappointment in himself upon realizing how little he really understood about this child who would be king.

CHAPTER 3

You Can Grow God-confident Children

As psychologists, sociologists, the news media and law enforcement officers work to unravel the mysteries of why in recent years children have chosen to become involved in violence like the Columbine school shootings, they've often uncovered the faces of young people who felt alienated and rejected by their peers. While there are undoubtedly many dynamics that led these troubled adolescents to do some of the terrible things we've watched unfolding on our TV screens, it's also certain that these adolescents somehow came to the conclusion that their lives – indeed life itself – were not valuable.

It can be a cold, cruel world that greets our children every time they step outside our homes, so it's imperative that we instill in each one the confidence that his life, his very essence, is valuable – to God and to us. Absorbing that truth early in life will help children develop a healthy sense of self-worth that will foster independence and self-control and see him through potential periods of alienation and rejection. While you as a parent do your best to prevent your child from prolonged periods of feeling like an outcast among his peers, you also create and become the safe haven where your child feels secure and valued.

Some Universal Human Needs

Curiously enough, one of the reasons gang membership is growing around the country at an alarming rate is because of a gang's ability to meet emotional needs for belonging, significance and meaning.

People of all ages, but children especially, need a sense of belonging. They must feel as though they fit in somewhere, that they have a special place in the midst of a particular people. Unfortunately, gangs have swelled their ranks with adolescents who longed to belong to some kind of group – and for some, eventually any kind will do. You can help your child immeasurably in life by, first of all, helping him understand how valuable his role and place in your own family is. As an intentional parent, you also can work to find a place where your child feels accepted outside the home. If it doesn't happen in the classroom, find a sports team or a club that accepts him. Keep looking for appropriate playmates with him where he can form friendships and acceptance.

Self-confidence begins with being confident in God

Children also need to feel *significant*. Their contribution to the group should be noted and approved. They don't have to be the star of the sports team, but their efforts have to count for something. Even better, when they learn that their influence makes an impact on the lives of others, they'll find true significance.

To understand that we live with purpose gives meaning to each of our lives. Children must learn what life is all about. Although most youngsters don't sit around philosophically debating the meaning of life, they do slowly start to understand that going through the motions of living is not enjoyable unless there is an understood purpose in them. They must begin to see their lives as part of a bigger picture. Frankly, outside of God this is very difficult – if not impossible – to achieve, so self-confidence begins with being confident in God.

You Do Belong

There are principles, bigger-than-life ideals, that we should impress on our children as soon as we become immersed in the parenting process. They are basic, fundamental truths that we must first embrace before we can turn them over to our kids.

Jeremiah 31:3 says, *I have loved you with an everlasting love; I have drawn you with loving-kindness.* This simple verse states some unequivocal truths that you – and your child – must understand. The first is quite simple yet overwhelming when we truly take it to heart.

God Loves You!

The Creator of the entire universe loves you. The one who made the oceans, the mountains, the moon and stars loves you! He cares deeply about everything that happens to you in your lifetime. Never forget that He was intimately involved in your creation. The psalmist understood this.

Yet to all who received him, to those who believe in his name, he gave the right to become children of God (John 1:12). Anyone who understands this supreme truth will always belong because he knows he has a place reserved in God's affections.

You Are Significant

In a world fascinated with celebrity, power and fortune, it's sometimes very easy to feel insignificant. So how do we convince the child who looks in the mirror and denigrates himself as too ordinary – the plain-faced, average student without any noticeable talent at first glance – that he is indeed special? If that describes your child, you probably don't have to be convinced yourself – but maybe you do. Perhaps you're in the middle of a "phase" that threatens to last forever with your child. You tell yourself he'll grow out of it – but in the meantime, secretly you wonder.

> Many things deemed "ordinary" by the world's measure may well be noble in God's eyes

Ecclesiastes 3:11 declares: *He has made everything beautiful in its time.* With this verse in mind, it really adds a new perspective to any "phase" your child may be going through. Isn't it good to know there is no part of childhood – not the terrible twos or even acne – that God won't redeem? Meanwhile, we should be reminded that many things deemed "ordinary" by the world's measure may well be noble in God's eyes.

Your Life Has Meaning

Figuring out our destinies is hard. Harder still perhaps is trying to lead your child to understand his. But discovering their talents and gifts, abilities and inclinations – all imperative – may be less important than recognizing and operating under the basic assumption that God has a special plan for his or her life.

Jeremiah 29:11 says: *"For I know the plans I have for you,"* declares the Lord, *"plans to prosper you and not to harm you, plans to give you hope and a future."* According to this verse, God already knows the purpose for your child's life.

Sometimes we squirm a little at the thought of putting ourselves under the Lord's control. We worry that we'll end up working out a plan that will be ill-suited to our capabilities or simply not enjoyable. But Jeremiah 29:11 promises us each a hope and a future if we conform to God's plan for our lives. We find our lives much more meaningful and fulfilling when we discover what it is that God wants us to do with them.

Unconditional Love

Once we as parents understand how much God loves us, it's our duty to exhibit that kind of love to our own children.

God said, *My command is this: Love each other as I have loved you* (John 15:12).

That is a promise from God in black and white. Often we find promises in Scripture that have conditions attached to them. To get what God has promised, we must keep our end of the bargain. There is no condition here. God does not ask us to earn His love. He does not tell us that if we mess up, He'll remove His love from us. Just the opposite! Love that has no limits is an unconditional love.

Paul said in Romans 8:38-39, *For I am convinced that neither death nor life, neither angels nor demons, neither the present nor the future, nor any powers, neither height nor depth, nor anything else in all creation will be able to separate us from the love of God that is in Christ Jesus our Lord.* His confidence that God loved him so complete he could make this ringing declaration.

Expressing Unconditional Love

Convinced that our children are valuable and important to God, how do we convey that to them? We act as a conduit, allowing God's unconditional love to be expressed to our children through us. In addition to pointing out to our children the biblical foundation for understanding God's love, we continually and intentionally demonstrate to them how valuable they are.

Psychologist Dr. Todd E. Linaman listed some practical things parents can do in *Ten Ways to Love your Children.*

1. *Provide for their physical needs.* Growing children need healthy diets, adequate clothing and quality health care. They need protection from harm – from "small stuff" like sunburn or too much junk food to real dangers like careless driving or access to alcohol or drugs.

2. *Be there for them.* When your children talk to you, face them and really listen. Turn off the TV if necessary. As much as possible, attend Little League games, school conferences or band concerts. Your presence, attention and availability will make a significant difference in their lives.

3. *Give them wings – and a net.* Let them try new things. You may fear that they will fail, but they need the opportunity to try to learn from that experience. Then be there to catch them when they fall and provide a landing place. You might just be surprised at how often they succeed.

4. *Balance individuality with absolutes.* You know your child is unique, so let him be different from

you. Celebrate individual strengths and try to see life from your child's perspective, showing respect for his personal preferences and fears. At the same time, never abandon your own convictions. Children need the security of immovable boundaries and guidelines for behavior. It's okay to prefer playing the violin to playing baseball, for example, but it's never okay to treat others with disrespect.

5. *Hold them accountable.* Children want to do right and be accepted. Communicate your expectations – and God's – then hold them accountable for them. If they have done wrong, encourage them to make amends. They might repair or replace a broken object, write an apology or perform community service. This restores self-respect and lets them know that their behaviors have consequences.

6. *Admit when you're wrong.* Let's face it, we as parents do make mistakes. Our kids intuitively know that too. If you're willing to say, "I blew it – I'm sorry," the children learn that the relationship is more important than maintaining the upper hand. It gives him the freedom to admit his mistakes as well. Facing the truth is a key to good emotional health.

7. *Love your spouse.* Children whose parents' marriage is stable are far more secure than those who are wondering if their world is about to fall apart. If you want your child to have a happy marriage later, he needs to see you weather storms with a commitment that supersedes personal comfort or happiness. Your children are happier when you put your spouse first and them second. If you are divorced, do your best to maintain a respectful relationship with the child's other parent.

8. ***Practice what you preach.*** That old adage, "actions speak louder than words," rings true. If you tell your kids not to lie then ask them to tell the salesman you're not home when he calls or ask them to respect their teachers while you badmouth your boss, don't expect good behavior reports at school conference time. And fight the temptation to drop them off at church – go with them!

9. ***Give physical affection.*** People need to be touched. Studies have shown that infants who are massaged thrive better than those left untouched. Children diagnosed with Attention Deficit Hyperactivity Disorder also respond to touch with calm. So lavish your child with appropriate forms of physical affection. As they grow older, take into consideration teenage sensibilities but never forget that they need touch, too.

10. ***Never give up on them!*** As our children grow up, some will make us proud and satisfied that we have done a good job. Others may make us wonder if we did anything right at all. The time comes when we have to back off and let them make their own decisions and mistakes. But you must never stop loving them and encouraging them to be the best they can be.

Encouraging Words

Solomon was the wisest man who ever lived – courtesy of God, who granted Solomon's wish for wisdom. His writings in the book of Proverbs are an illustration of how to raise God-confident children. Affectionately addressing "my son," Solomon gives practical advice and teaches God's precepts. His instructions were so detailed and his longing for his son to live a good, righteous life – and avoid the pitfalls – was so evident that he also manages to convey the depth of a father's love for a child. If Solomon's son gave as much thought to Proverbs as Solomon did, he not only had confidence in God's love for him – but Solomon's.

CHAPTER 4

There is a Reason Behind Misbehavior

Kerry will always remember the afternoon she invited another mother and daughter to join her and daughter, Katie, for lunch. The other child was almost the same age as Katie so cultivating a friendship with them seemed natural. As they sat around the dining table, Kerry took special pains to draw the other child out, laughing in delight as she answered a question with winsome charm. Her laughter turned into a gasp, when suddenly, inexplicably, Katie reached across the table and pulled the other child's hair.

"Why did you do that?" Kerry demanded in utter astonishment. To her knowledge, her daughter had never behaved that way before, even when provoked. What had just happened here?

Do you remember ever doing something which you understood was unacceptable but without understanding quite why you were doing it? There's a simple reason why children – and adults – misbehave. The Bible identifies it as our sin nature. Unfortunately, each of us is born with a natural tendency to act wrongly. The psalmist explained it this way, *Surely I was sinful at birth, sinful from the time my mother conceived me* (Psalm 51:5). Obviously, a tiny baby doesn't willfully commit acts of sin, so what the psalmist was concluding is that we have inherited a flaw that will catch up with us eventually. We misbehave because it's in our human nature to do so.

It wasn't always that way, of course. The biblical account of creation reveals that mankind *chose* sin (see Genesis 3), but once that happened, there was no turning back.

It is sin that separates us from God, according to Romans 3:23. And it is that sin that prompted God to send Jesus to us. 2 Corinthians 5:21 says, *God made him who had no sin to be sin for us, so that in him we might become the righteousness of God.* As you can see, our sin tendency doesn't have to be a fatal flaw – not as long as we accept that Jesus paid the price for it!

But that tendency toward sin does have to be mastered – or at the very least, controlled – because not only will it separate us from God, it has the power to alienate everyone else too. After all, God loves us unconditionally and is very patient with our shortcomings. But you just try being a friend to someone who pulls your hair at the dinner table for no good reason!

If you've spent a lifetime learning to control your sinful impulses and habits, you undoubtedly already understand the importance of helping your child onto the path of righteousness by teaching her how to recognize good from evil and make right choices.

In the last chapter we learned that one of the important factors in raising God-confident children is helping them develop a sense of belonging and significance. In his popular book, *Children: The Challenge* [1], psychiatrist and author Rudolf Dreikurs observed that children who are unable to fulfill their need for belonging in positive ways often become discouraged and ultimately begin to display negative behaviors.[1] Before long, these children learn that their misbehavior can have a greater payoff than following the rules or cooperating. According to Dreikurs, the child's goals of misbehavior fall into four general categories: attention, power, revenge and displaying inadequacy.

> Kids often use misbehavior as attention-seeking devices, although they may not know that's why they're doing it

Attention

Why did Katie attack the little girl who was suddenly claiming so much of her mother's attention? Might she have been jealous? Could it be that Katie's outburst was a ploy, albeit probably unconscious, to draw mom's attention to her own little darling – where Katie thought it rightfully belonged?

Kids often use misbehavior as attention-seeking devices, although they may not know that's why they're doing it. They may not even be justified in seeking and demanding more attention. But just the same, they may act out as a way to get the adults or other children in the room to look their way.

Power

Many misbehaviors stem from that age-old desire for power. Consider the example of Tyrone. He whimpered every time he was put to bed at 8 p.m. on the dot. His mother, who had quit her job to stay home with him, was pretty sure that it wasn't her attention he craved. She had a sneaking suspicion that perhaps her husband's busy schedule was causing Tyrone to act this way. Maybe he just wasn't getting enough of his father's attention. To soothe him, sometimes she turned the light back on, rocked Tyrone, or read him stories until he finally fell asleep.

---

[1] Rudolf Dreikurs and Vickie Soltz, Children: The Challenge (New York: Dutton, 1987)

When the crying didn't abate, Tyrone's mom and dad eventually decided to re-assign the bedtime chores. Tyrone's dad volunteered to oversee the boy's bath, read the story and say the prayers before the lights went out – but he still screamed, night after night. It wasn't attention he sought. It was control. Tyrone wanted power over his bedtime. And only when that 8 p.m. curfew was consistently enforced, night after night, did he finally accept defeat, learn to roll over and go quietly to sleep.

Misbehavior is often a power struggle in disguise. Parents have been given the responsibility of guiding their children's lives, but in what areas might you want your child to exercise more control as he ages?

Don't forget that admonition to parents in Ephesians 6:4, *Fathers, do not exasperate your children; instead, bring them up in the training and instruction of the Lord.* Parents can be guilty of engaging in needless power struggles with children, overburdening them with too many demands. Strive for balance.

Revenge

Some of the misbehavior is actually a direct response to situations where children feel overpowered. Then they're ready for revenge. For example, they don't like their teachers so they deliberately try to disrupt classroom lectures or submit to their impulses to talk too much.

_____ ⁓ _____
Knowing why a child misbehaves may be an aid to helping him control that behavior

Fifteen year-old Riley was very upset when he learned that his dad was accepting a work transfer that would take him away from his friends and school. He listened to the reasons why this move was imperative – his father would lose his job altogether if he refused to transfer – but Riley blamed his parents for caving into pressure. When a classmate at his new school offered him a beer at a party one night, he accepted it in defiance of the warnings from his parents against drinking. "If they don't care about me, why should I care about them?" was his reasoning. Riley wanted his parents to suffer as much as he was, and he'd found a way.

Knowing why a child misbehaves may be an aid to helping him control that behavior. In Riley's case, the unwanted move was very traumatic.

Display of Inadequacy

The fourth goal is used by a child who is feeling very discouraged in life. This child may have learned through a series of life experiences that their attempts to measure up are simply not good enough. This is a child who believes it is better to no longer even try, than to try and fail. According to Rudolf Dreikurs, "A completely discouraged child gives up entirely: he feels that he has no chance to succeed in any way, be it by useful or useless means. He becomes helpless and uses his helplessness, exaggerating any real or imagined weakness or deficiency, to avoid any task where his expected failure may be even more embarrassing. The seemingly stupid child is frequently a discouraged child who uses his stupidity as a means of avoiding any effort whatsoever."

Take the case of 15-year-old Steven. He has never done very well in school. In fact, his mother often tells him, as well as others, that he is one of those children who will be better off learning a trade rather than going to college. In his freshman year of high school Steven started ditching classes. His already poor grades began declining even more. Now in his sophomore year Steven is talking about dropping out of school altogether because he says he can't learn anyway. He has admitted to "experimenting" with drugs and alcohol. His mother often finds herself saying, "I give up. I just don't know what else I can do for Steven."

This type of response to a child's behavior is often a clear indication that the goal of the child is to convince those around him that he is not worth their effort to try and change him because he is a hopeless case. After all, if he's incompetent, he can avoid the difficult challenges of life, right?

Don't ignore
negative behavior

"That's Life" Discipline to the Rescue

Knowing why your child misbehaves gives you valuable insight in knowing how to respond. For example, a child who screams for attention may very well be providing vital clues that he is in some way being neglected. On the other hand, a child screaming for attention also might be telling you that he's much inclined to be selfish and narcissistic and has already been given way too much. It's your job as parent to figure out the best course of action in response to your child's behavior.

But what you don't want to do is simply ignore negative behavior. As soon as you're aware of a problem you must deal with it – or the behavior may just take on a life of its own and flourish. The Bible supports this, *He who spares the rod hates his son, but he who loves him is careful to discipline him* (Proverbs 13:24). Parents who truly love their child discipline them.

Negative Behavior Ignored Compounds!

Ignoring negative behavior without teaching consequences frustrates our children. If overburdening our children can "exasperate them" as Ephesians 6:4 warns, failing to show them the boundaries and limits of life will frustrate them, too. When we as parents ignore negative behavior we may inadvertently send our child into a cycle of failure.

Instead, teach your child that negative behaviors have real consequences. We call this *"That's Life" Discipline.* It's a simple concept. Let real life consequences of a child's mis-behavior catch up with him. If you can't see obvious natural consequences, take action so that there will be logical con-sequences. Let's look at our previous examples.

Katie got jealous of her mom's attention and pulled another child's hair in a fit of resentment. The logical consequence is that Katie is removed from the dining table and placed in timeout in her room. Now she has learned that particular negative behavior did not reward her with the attention she sought. Just the opposite! Now Katie doesn't get the com-pany of either her mother or new friend. That's life!

What about Tyrone? Being left screaming in your bed night after night is a natural consequence to a refusal to submit to his parents' desires that he get a good night's sleep. Scream-ing really isn't a lot of fun. Snuggling quietly into a warm bed and soft pillow is much more pleasurable. Tyrone will figure that out – especially when his parents make sure he still gets up at the same time each morning. That's life!

Riley is another story. What are the poor, guilt-ridden parents to do when they catch their teenager drinking after having turned their child's world upside down themselves? How about holding him accountable for breaking their rules – and the law! Riley will need some extra help coping in his new environment, finding new friends and developing a support system there. He needs reassurance that his parents care for him. Loving words and extra attention will be very important. But parents who love their child won't shrug off an incident involving alcohol. Riley will have to learn that living on the edge away from home results in being kept at home. That's life!

The parents of Steven the 15-year-old, who wants to give up on school, may convince themselves that the situation is hopeless and there is nothing they can do to hold him accountable for his behavior. In this case, the parents would be wise to seek professional help for their son, but that is not all they can do. If Steven refuses to attend class or is determined to continue his drug and alcohol use, his parents can agree – and make it clear to him – that they won't

Remember that discipline is not an angry, knee-jerk response to a child's misbehavior

interfere with the possible consequences associated with his illegal behavior. In other words, if he is arrested for drugs or truancy, they will not bail him out. A logical consequence for dropping out of school may involve requiring him to find a full-time job and begin contributing financially to the family. That's life!

Knowing that each of us possesses the potential to do wrong will help us as parents deal with it as it happens. But just as our children are individuals, so is effective discipline. It goes back to the importance of knowing and understanding your child. If Molly is a homebody, putting her on restriction may not be an effective way to discipline her. But if Molly despises yard work, you have a tool to use in molding future behaviors.

Remember that discipline is not an angry, knee-jerk response to a child's misbehavior. It is a well thought out prayerful plan of action.

It's important to note here that reinforcing positive behaviors is an effective tool as well. Lavishly affirm your children when they choose positive behaviors over negative ones. We must be diligent about being aware of the times when our children make good choices, especially when they've been tempted otherwise. Flattery (praise that is not earned) will not do the trick. We have to look for those opportunities that will actually encourage our children toward righteousness.

A word aptly spoken is like apples of gold in settings of silver (Proverbs 25:11).

Wise words are precious gifts. Whether they are words of correction, counsel or affirmation, when we use timely situations to train our children, we are preparing them to make good choices in the future.

No matter how careful and consistent you are in teaching your child, expect that she will mess up on occasion. Some behaviors take more time to get under control than others do. Remind yourself of that the fourteenth time your child "forgets" to do his homework. If, instead of becoming discouraged or resigned to a child's tendency toward a particular sin, you apply intentional, effective discipline, eventually it will come under control…at least most of the time. Meanwhile, comfort yourself with the words of the Apostle Paul, who admitted that he never quite achieved the level of self-control he desired, *I do not understand what I do. For what I want to do I do not do, but what I hate I do* (Romans 7:15).

Angling for Attention

When Jacob's sons committed the abominable act of selling their young brother Joseph into slavery (Genesis 37:1-36), they were utilizing a terrible way to get something they wanted: attention. His brothers were jealous of Joseph because they wanted the attention their father reserved for him. Of course, as we know, this atrocity never achieved what they unconsciously wanted – even though they tried to comfort their father and replace Joseph in his affections, Jacob grieved on.

Meanwhile, the brothers had to live with what they did. The Bible doesn't record them, but there were probably previous signs that the brothers' misbehaviors stemmed from a desire for attention. We would not have the wonderful story of Joseph to inspire us on what it means to forgive if things had been different, but Jacob may not have ever missed so much of Joseph's life if he'd given all his sons proper attention.

CHAPTER 5

You Must Play the Entire Game

It probably wasn't an entirely accurate assessment (no-
body's perfect), but Sylvia and Jake thought of their
daughter Brooke as the model child – right up until about
age 11. In sixth grade, suddenly things seemed different.
Brooke seemed different. Their sweet, lovable little girl
behaved, well… not so sweetly these days. In fact, she was
cranky – a lot of the time. And instead of dutifully obeying
every command that Sylvia and Jake uttered without question, Brooke now tended to challenge their dictates. Why
was this necessary…and what good would that do?

Sylvia and Jake were at first flabbergasted. Then as time
passed and Brooke's disposition didn't improve (in fact, it
got worse) they were continually disappointed and, (truth
be known) getting angry themselves. In their hearts they
yearned for the old days when Brooke simply did as she was
told. In time they grew a little fearful, too. What was happening to their daughter – and their lives?

Two Halves Make the Whole

In case you haven't given it much thought, let us be the first
to encourage you to do it now. Like a basketball game, there
are two halves to parenting. If you're a sports fan maybe
you've noticed that the pace and momentum of the game

often shifts after half time – sometimes radically. The team that was winning in the first half comes back on the court looking a little tired. On the other hand, the losing team seems to have used the break to gain a new edge in attitude. Suddenly, they're on the winning side.

So it is with parenting. Just as you get used to the rhythm of the game, maybe even congratulating yourself on being on the winning side, you realize that life has shifted. You're in the second half of parenting, and you hadn't even noticed until your child started throwing shots that you'd never seen before.

Good coaches use half time to review game strategy and make appropriate adjustments in play. Before you move into the second half of parenting, be prepared with a game plan. Successful parenting requires making a strong showing through the whole game, and often a strategy adjustment is required at half time.

Clues that Half-time is Approaching

The first half of parenting is built around rules – a code of conduct that needs to be established early in a child's life and enforced often. During the first half, at times you must use more control over your child than during the second half of parenting. You draw up a rulebook, a set of standards that you expect your child to live up to so she can be in proper relation with God, you as a parent and others. You lovingly insist on her adhering to the code of conduct by setting limits and teaching discipline.

The second half of parenting requires a switch in focus

In a lot of ways, parenting in the first half can be a particularly pleasurable job because your child will let you hold her close while you do it. She sits on your lap while you read with her. She runs back to get one last hug before heading off to a sleepover. You realize that you really like this part of parenting, this holding on. You cherish every precious moment. Once you got the hang of setting boundaries and enforcing them, it was easy.

The second half of parenting requires a switch in focus. The emphasis on rules no longer seems to be working. The focus must now settle on relationship. In the second half of parenting you must learn to trust your child's judgment regarding conduct. Instead of control, you now hope to influence your child's behavior while feeding your child's self-determination. For the most part, the training phase is over, giving way to the second half when you must begin the process of letting go as your child journeys toward adulthood. When do you make this parenting transition from rules to relationship? You'll know half time is fast approaching from the following clues:

- *Your child's age.* For both boys and girls, things start changing around age 9 or 10, the onset of adolescence. Many parents see adolescence as a necessary evil, a stage to be endured, but taking that attitude will short-change your pleasure in the parenting ballgame. The game changes, yes, but never forget that your child is becoming the person God intended and needs you now more than ever – even if she refuses to sit with you while you read stories.

- *You feel a loss of control.* You feel it because it's really happening. You are no longer the center of your child's universe. Friends and other activities will take on a higher priority than family.

- *The rulebook is changing.* Telling your child to obey "because I said so" doesn't work anymore. This "thinking" being wants to know why – and the answers had better be good ones.

- *You hear yourself saying, "He didn't use to be like this."* And he didn't. Maturation has started and a different child is emerging because of it.

Play the Entire Game

A strong leader thinks ahead of his followers. In the same way, a good parent thinks ahead of their child. You need to have a game plan for the first half. Understand the unique bent of your son or daughter and give him or her a healthy sense of worth. Raise them to be God-confident in the first half. Remember that kids believe what they're told by adults.

Then when half time comes, make the necessary adjustments. Use common sense and be ready to apply Scripture according to the particular bent of your child. Have positive expectations for your teenager, but be flexible. If you don't bend, you'll break. Pick your battles carefully and nurture your relationship with your child.

Decide before the second half which standards are non-negotiable and which you'll be willing to be flexible about

And keep at it. We can grow very complacent and think we've got the parenting thing all figured out when things are going smoothly. But it's as we grow inattentive that we make mistakes. So mentally prepare for the long haul. And think ahead.

Remember your Creator in the days of your youth,
before the days of trouble come and the years ap-
proach when you will say, I find no pleasure in
them" – before the sun and the light and the moon
and the stars grow dark, and the clouds return af-
ter the rain; when the keepers of the house tremble,
and the strong men stoop, when the grinders cease
because they are few, and those looking through
the windows grow dim; when the doors to the
street are closed and the sound of the grinding
fades; when men rise up at the sound of birds, but
all their sounds grow faint; when men are afraid
of heights and of dangers in the streets; when the
almond tree blossoms and the grasshopper drags
himself along and desire no longer is stirred. Then
man goes to his eternal home and mourners go
about the streets. Remember him – before the
silver cord is severed, or the gold bowl is broken;
before the pitcher is shattered at the spring, or the
wheel broken at the well, and the dust returns to
the ground it came from, and the spirit returns to
God, who gave it. Ecclesiastes 12:1-7

Doesn't the second half of parenting sound like fun? Actually a good sense of humor will go a long way in helping you cope. So most certainly will prayer. As you can see, you need to decide even before your child hits the second half which standards are non-negotiable in your house and which you'll be willing to be flexible about.

Know that your child will not choose as you would prefer in every case. Before giving in on a particular issue ask yourself these questions to help you decide if this is a battle you'll want to fight:

✓ Would this action be spiritually detrimental to my child?

✓ Would it harm his physical health?

✓ Why am I concerned about this issue?

✓ Is there biblical instruction on this topic?

✓ What is the worst-case scenario if I give in on this issue? How likely is a worst-case scenario?

When in doubt, seek the counsel of other parents, pastors, a trusted mentor or professionals. Ask your child to go with you to get their input. Remind him that counsel is just that – seeking the advice of someone else to help you make a good decision. Promise your child that you will pray about your decision. Ask your child to do the same. Read James 1:5 together: *If any of you lacks wisdom he should ask God.*

Keep in mind while good common sense and godly wisdom usually dictate a typical response, you also have to consider the individuality of your own child in deciding your course of action.

Trying to determine a course of action for the second half now may put you ahead of the game, but be prepared to make those half-time adjustments. Parents of young children often have idealistic standards for parenting teens. When you finish this study, tuck this book away until you're in the second half, if you're not there already. Then try out those scenarios again to see if you've made some half-time adjustments.

It's Not Over as Long as You Need to Blow the Whistle

Perhaps no one came to understand how long the parenting game might last and the importance of staying focused in the second half more than the prophet Eli. Even though Eli's sons had achieved manhood, they still needed guidance. Knowing that they were practicing grave evils, Eli took them to task for their wickedness. While his words were ignored, this incident shows that the task of parenting extends well beyond early childhood. Apparently no one else bothered to confront Eli's sons with their wickedness – and his rebuke was too little, too late. Eli knew that at this point that their sins were really between them and God, but they couldn't say they hadn't been warned. Hophni and Phinehas paid the ultimate price for their rebellion – death – and Eli lost favor with God for dropping the ball (1 Samuel 2:12-36). Their story is a lesson for every parent who's ready to quit at half time.

CHAPTER 6

Understanding Your Parenting Style

Brenda is a single parent of two boys. She's been raising them on her own since she and her husband divorced when the boys were toddlers and she got sole custody. Brenda decided soon after her husband left that she would make sure the boys understood that the absence of a male authority in the home did not mean the absence of all authority.

Through the years Brenda has taken pains to make sure that the boys knew who was in control. She taught them that questioning her decisions was taboo. They were to be obedient to her demands whenever she spoke. She knew that some of her friends considered her a pretty hard taskmaster, but she countered that with a pretty good argument: "If you were a single mother of boys, you would have to be, too. Give them an inch and they'll take a mile." Brenda didn't care how much whining her children did or how often her friends weighed in with their counsel. Her word was law.

Shelley waited a long time to have a baby. She and her husband struggled with infertility for ten years before treatments yielded results. Shelley was thrilled to finally be the mother of a daughter, and it showed! Everyone could tell how much she loved that "little angel," especially little Lola herself. As she grew, Lola realized that her mom loved her so much she had trouble refusing her anything. Dad was another story, so Lola soon learned whom to approach first when she wanted her way. Not that Shelley spoiled her child – of that she was quite sure. She just had a softer side; she would remind herself when husband Dick seemed disappointed in a parenting decision that she made without consulting him.

"I'm not sure Lola should be allowed to do that yet," Dick would object.

"But she's a really good child," Shelley would counter. And she was. Lola had given them no real problems.

Linda and Jack realized early on that their parenting styles tended to differ. Linda had a strong parental role model in her own father, so she tended to lean heavily on her authority. Jack, on the other hand, realized he was something of a soft touch. When his two young daughters smiled at him, his heart melted.

For example, when their youngest asked Linda if she could go to a birthday party for a neighborhood child at the mall arcade, Linda turned her down flat. She didn't know the family, she explained, so that was that. Linda was impervious to her daughter's pleas.

But the day after the party, while she was at church, Linda realized she'd made a mistake. Of course, she knew the birthday girl. This was a family she'd met and invited to church herself. They were new to the community and inviting Linda's daughter to the birthday bash was one of the ways they'd been trying to make their own child find friends in her new environment. In fact, they'd invited a handful of kids in the neighborhood. No one had come.

Linda was embarrassed – especially when Jack reminded her that the mother had mentioned that their daughter would receive an invitation. She'd simply forgotten the new family's last name. If she had consulted Jack – who remembered them well – or asked more questions from the start, she would have been happy to let their daughter go.

The best parenting decisions are made together

Likewise, Jack had made his own poor parenting decisions. He had been watching the girls one afternoon when a neighborhood boy stopped by and asked their oldest daughter to play ping-pong with him at his house. Jack readily gave his permission.

He was embarrassed when he got a phone call a couple of hours later from the boy's mother. She'd just gotten home from work. She apologized for her son's issuing an invitation to his daughter in her absence. She explained that she would talk to her son about that. Jack soon realized that his daughter had been in this boy's home without adult supervision – something he would have immediately vetoed if he'd asked a few more questions.

Because of situations like these, Linda and Jack soon realized that their best parenting decisions were made together. Linda still tended to lean on the side of authority while Jack was inclined to be trusting, but together they made a good team. When Jack allowed the relationship to take first priority, Linda reminded him of the rules. When Linda focused on the rules, Jack reminded her of how responsible their girls were. They learned to ask each other: "What do you think?" and find some accord.

Would you agree that Brenda, Sarah, Linda and Jack are all parents who want to be responsible? Is there a single one of them that you would classify as negligent, unloving or inadequate?

On the contrary, Brenda, Sarah, Linda and Jack are all conscientious parents who love their children and want the best for them. Despite being intentional, each are fallible (as are we all), and each has a parenting style that influences their decision-making, sometimes leading them to illogical or dubious choices.

Each of us as parents has the potential to adopt a style that tends to lead us into making parental decisions almost by rote. According to Dr. Rudolf Dreikurs in his classic book, *Children: The Challenge*, styles of parenting can be broken down into three basic categories: authoritarian (or dictatorial), permissive and authoritative.

Parenting styles

"My Way." The authoritarian parent tends to control the child's activity according to rigid standards of behavior. An authoritarian parent stresses obedience, de-emphasizes collaboration and dialogue, and employs strong forms of punishment to deter unwanted behavior.

"Your Way." The permissive parent tends to make few demands and avoids exercising control while leaving their children to govern their own behavior. Permissive parents often refrain from setting firm boundaries and giving their children the guidance they need.

"Our Way." The authoritative parent directs the child's activities in a relational, relatively flexible way, encouraging collaboration and dialogue yet exercising authority when necessary.

In her book *Discipline Them, Love Them*, Betty Chase offers some more clues to parenting styles.[2] According to Chase, the authoritarian parent does not respect the child's opinions, feelings and needs; obedience is more important than

---

[2] Chase, Betty, *Discipline Them, Love Them* (Cook, 1992)

relationship. The authoritarian parent spends little time listening to the child and offers little emotional support.

The permissive parent lets the child do as he pleases, leaving him with too many choices and too little guidance. When the child doesn't behave, the permissive parent may plead with the child for obedience rather than forcing it.

The authoritative parent believes a child is immature and needs direction. The authoritative parent requires obedience because he knows what's best for the child. At the same time, he spends time with the child, listens, and is very concerned about meeting the child's needs and helping him develop to his fullest potential.

Chase also identifies a fourth category of parenting, the neglectful parent. If you're reading this book, you can probably eliminate yourself from this style of parenting. This is the parent who just doesn't care – or doesn't care enough to improve their parenting skills. By virtue of spending time in this study, you've already demonstrated that you do.

The Ideal Parent

Perhaps you've reached the conclusion that, according to these definitions, the ideal parent is the authoritative parent. This is the parent who has a lot of control over his child while consistently and unconditionally loving and supporting him. This parent is a firm, effective disciplinarian with a soft side. Sound appealing? Sound *impossible*?

Keep in mind that while you may have a parenting style or tendency to parent in a certain way, that doesn't mean you're bound to stay in that mold forever. Often we start out parenting in a certain style because that's the way we were parented. We simply follow the generational model.

Think back to your own childhood. Can you identify your

parents' styles? Understanding your natural tendencies also will help you improve your style. You can build on your strengths and work on your weaknesses.

Ahead you will find three more scenarios. See if you can identify the parenting style displayed.

Sarah came into the kitchen where mom was fixing breakfast. She played with a pencil on the counter and meekly said, "Mom, all the kids are going to the mall after school today. Shannon's brother, Ben, will drive us there and pick us up at seven and bring us home. Can I go?"

Mom didn't look up from stirring the orange juice and answered: "Absolutely not! You know that you may not ride in a car with someone we don't know."

"But, Mom," Sarah pleaded, "Ben's a junior this year. He's on the basketball team and in Student Senate. He's very responsible."

"You know the rules. And I've already said no."

"Please, Mom! I'll be the only one in our group who's not there! It's so embarrassing! I don't care what you say – I'm going!"

"Don't talk back to me, Sarah! This subject is closed. I'll determine when and where you go, and you're not going anywhere because you're grounded!"

Recognize this style?

"Mom, all the kids are going to the mall after school. Shannon's brother said he'd take us and pick us up. Can I go?"

Sarah's mom was concerned. "I don't know Shannon's brother. I really prefer for you to only ride with people we know."

"But I do know him, Mom – I see him all the time at Shannon's house. He's a responsible guy – it'll be okay. Can I go? Please!"

"Well, I don't feel good about it…but I guess it's okay. I want you home by six, though, understand?"

"Six? That's so early! Can't I just come home when Ben comes for Shannon? After all, they're giving me a ride, and I can't tell them when to pick me up. That would be rude."
Sarah's mother shrugged. "Well, maybe just this one time."

Have you got this style pegged?

After hearing her daughter's request to ride to the mall with a driver unknown to her, Sarah's mother says: "Sarah, I'm concerned about a couple things. First we've agreed that you're not to ride in a car with anyone we don't know. Second, I'm concerned about your being at the mall for such a long period of time. There can be trouble when a group of kids is hanging around unsupervised."

"But, Mom, I know Ben. He's Shannon's brother. Anyway, I don't want to be the only one who can't go – that's not fair!"

"I don't want to be unfair, but I also don't want you to be in a situation where neither you nor I have control."

"Can't I ride with Ben this once? It'll be okay."

"No, Sarah. If you want to meet your friends at the mall, I can drop you off and pick you up a couple of hours later."

Sarah is momentarily disappointed. "Okay, but if I bring Ben over to meet you and Dad, will you let me ride with him and Shannon sometime?"

"We'll see. We would like to meet Ben, but I can't make any promises yet."

If you've identified your personal parenting style as too authoritarian or too permissive, you may be feeling like a parental failure next to the authoritative parent (a.k.a. Super Parent). Never fear. God really isn't asking you to be a Super Parent. He knows all about your tendencies and failings. After all, He's forgiven them for years. Moreover, even if you are a single parent or both spouses bring only one parenting style to a family, you're not in this business of child rearing alone. You have the ultimate parent to turn to when you need help – God.

Exercising Authority

Not only were Mary and Joseph raising the perfect child, Jesus, but also, as it turns out, they were pretty good parents themselves. We know that Mary was a student of Jesus – she pondered in her heart all that He said and did – but she and Joseph assumed an authoritative style of parenting that worked well with this special child. We get a look at it in Luke 2:41-52 during an incident when Jesus drifted away from His family to linger at the temple.

Mary and Joseph were right to hold Jesus accountable for staying behind without permission. But they also seemed to listen when Jesus explained that He had a higher authority. They still demanded obedience – and got it, according to Luke 2:51 – but they apparently also took into account that they were raising a very special child.

CHAPTER 7

Your Part in Creating a Vision for Your Child

If you've accepted that children don't come with instruction manuals, but find yourself longing for one anyhow, there may be a point to your dreaming. You'll never come up with a set of day-to-day how-tos that will see you through child rearing – but you can come up with guidelines that will shape your daily parenting and help your child reach his potential.

As God breathed life into your child, your dreams for his future started taking shape. Now as you help your child learn how to properly relate to God and his fellow man, and utilize individual strengths, gifts and talents, they take wings. In other words, creating a vision for your child means coming up with a plan to follow for intentional parenting. The more you think, pray and plan for your child, the larger the vision. But for dreams to come true, every aspect must be in line with God's vision for your child.

Start with *the* principle

Let's go back to God's vision of the model child, Jesus. According to Luke 2: 52, *Jesus grew in wisdom and stature, and in favor with God and men.* Our relationship with God will greatly affect our ability to relate to others. Therefore, nurturing your child's relationship with God will help your child be in right relation with others, including you, siblings, a future spouse, other relatives, friends and co-workers. Check the box below if you desire this to be a part of your vision for your child.

❏   I want my child to hunger for God and have a relationship with Him that sustains him through life.

How can you help create this hunger for God in your child's life? Here are seven ONE THINGS you can do to help your child develop a relationship with God, keeping in mind his unique personality. Check off each one you are willing to do. Choose the most important "one thing" to practice starting today. Once you become consistent in that, do the next right ONE THINGS on the list.

❏   I will tell my child how important my own relationship to God is.

❏   I will take my child to church.

❏   I will show my child the effects of having a relationship with God in my own life.

❏   I will make sure my child meets other godly people who are genuine, interesting and impressive.

❏   I will choose a church that truly understands how important children are to God. As my child becomes a teenager, I will ensure that adolescents receive proper discipleship opportunities.

❏   I will demonstrate godliness to my child myself, beginning with keeping my promises.

❏   I will show my child the unconditional love that God gives me.

And the Second is Like unto It

Now let's take a look at another relationship. As you may recall, how we treat our fellow man is second in importance only to the way we treat our Creator, according to Matthew 22:37-39. Other Scripture gives even more insight into the interdependence of these two concepts.

> *We love because he first loved us. If anyone says, "I love God," yet hates his brother, he is a liar. For anyone who does not love his brother, whom he has seen, cannot love God, whom he has not seen. And he has given us this command: Whoever loves God must also love his brother.*
> 1 John 4:19-21

According to this, if we do not love our fellow man, we cannot truly love God. It's impossible to truly love God yet hate what He loves – and He loves the whole world, according to John 3:16.

After having looked at some of the reasons why children misbehave, we know that we must teach them to behave properly. We've already discovered that there are steps to learning how to be a good citizen.

Learning to obey parents teaches children how to be submissive to authorities later in life by giving them experience controlling their desires

Exodus 20:3-17 tells us that the primary responsibility of childhood is to honor your father and mother. Learning to obey parents teaches children how to be submissive to authorities later in life by giving them experience controlling their desires. Here are some ONE THINGS you can do to see that part of the vision for your child to be a loving and contributing member of society fulfilled. Check off each one you are willing to do. Choose the most important ONE THING to practice starting today. Once you become consistent in that, do the next right ONE THING on the list.

- ❑ I will teach my child God's Word.

- ❑ I will model submission to authorities myself.

- ❑ I will correct my child to help him learn obedience.

If you want your children to learn God's Word you're going to need a plan to accomplish that, remembering that in the second half your game plan might need to be adjusted. Check the ONE THINGS you think will work for you and your family right now. Be prepared to make changes as your child grows.

- ❑ I will read the Bible with my child.

- ❑ I will provide age-appropriate materials that enhance Bible study.

- ❑ I will take my child to church where he can hear more of God's word.

- ❑ I will tell my child about my experiences, which apply God's Word in my own life.

- ❑ I will discuss God's Word as it applies to my child's daily experiences.

The Wisdom to Know the Difference

Knowing God's Word and applying it can be entirely different things. Someone can be very conscientious without ever being courageous. In other words, exemplary responsible adults not only have a strong value system but the courage to act on it. All of us are faced with decisions in our lives where we get to choose between better and best. If we want the best for our children, then they have to learn to distinguish it from the assortment of other options.

We already learned that the fear of God is the beginning of wisdom. In Philippians 4:6-7, the Apostle Paul reminds us that we can have peace by taking anxiety-producing problems and decisions to God. Would you agree that teaching your child to pray is an important part of parenting? Check the "one things" that you think will help your child make wise choices throughout his lifetime.

- ❏ I will pray with my child before meals.

- ❏ I will pray with my child before bedtime.

- ❏ I will pray with my child before events that cause him anxiety, like starting a new school or taking a test.

- ❏ My child will see me and my spouse praying together.

- ❏ We will pray as a family about decisions that affect all of us, including practical things like whether to buy a new car or living room furniture.

- ❏ We will pray with our child about key parenting decisions.

Companions for the Journey

Our children will need support from others to get through life, but we must realize that some others also have the power to throw them off track, where the threat of losing their way is dangerously real. Although God has the ability to redeem any situation or problem and work it to His glory (Romans 8:28), He also is a God who practices justice and allows us to live with the consequences of our bad choices.

If we live righteously, we are the best models our child will have, and our example will make profound impact on his choices. Take comfort in that and invest yourself in your child's life accordingly.

But no one lives in a vacuum. And none of us can keep our child cocooned from the world forever – nor should we. But we can hope that the people they come in contact with will bring out the best in them instead of the worst. We want our children to have good friends who will support and love him and help him reach his potential.

Your child will connect with certain people in his lifetime simply because he is the unique creation that you're discovering him to be. But others will appear in his life – or disappear – because you as a parent have taken pains to introduce your child to people who will enrich him – and to remove those who are bad influences. Usually you can take steps to do the latter without being overly controlling or heavy-handed. But in a few dire cases, direct intervention may be needed.

The ultimate responsibility for individual behavior lies with the individual

Did you read the account of Cassie Bernall, a Christian teenager slain in the Columbine school shootings?[3] Cassie's parents were quick to point out that their own daughter might have been headed down the same path as the shooters if they had not taken drastic action when they saw problems.

After reading some letters where their lives were threatened, this couple forced their daughter to change schools and cut

[3]Misty Bernall, She said Yes: The Unlikely Martyrdom of Cassie Bernall (Nashville: Wor

off dubious friendships that they suspected were introducing her to or compounding her destructive habits.

Let's be clear on this point: the ultimate responsibility for individual behavior lies with the individual. But sometimes others can become obstacles in our paths. As Cassie's parents saw their daughter's decline into an obsession with the dark side, they knew they had to get rid of the obstacles, including friends with a negative influence.

If you know the rest of the story, you have heard that when their daughter died, she died not as another sad statistic of troubled teenagers, but was heralded as a Christian martyr for the faith she expressed at gunpoint. Did Cassie Bernall fulfill her parent's vision for her? One has to assume that in her short life, she ultimately did.

Here are some ONE THINGS you do to help your children find and develop good friends.

- ❏   I will consistently and persistently pray for good friends for my children.

- ❏   I will look for appropriate companions for my children and try to cultivate relationships with them.

- ❏   I will allow my home to be a place where other children are welcome.

- ❏   When children are in my home, I will monitor their activities.

- ❏   I will always try to appreciate the good qualities in my children's friends, but I will exercise the right to intervene appropriately when I see signs of problems.

❏   I will pay attention to the key adults in my child's life, including grandparents and teachers, nurturing relationships and ensuring that they stay healthy.

Boundaries Along the Way

The relationships your child will have with the opposite sex are some of the most important – and potentially the most damaging. Every parent fears the problems adolescents create for themselves when they engage in sex outside of marriage. Beyond the potential physical problems – disease and pregnancy – there are emotional repercussions that can be ignored for a while but never fully escaped.

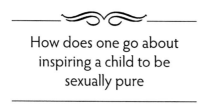

How does one go about inspiring a child to be sexually pure

In addition, sexual sin is only one of the great temptations facing our children. Alcohol and drug use and smoking all loom as temptations to young people – and great threats to their health for years to come.

How does one go about inspiring a child to be sexually pure in an era of sexually explicit movies and videos routinely depicting adults and even teenagers in sexual relationships outside of marriage ? How do we as parents instill a value in our child about the immorality of sex before marriage or the dangers of smoking for example? How do we begin to suggest that alcohol and drug use is immoral when it also is glorified in society? There are some things you can do, beginning with guiding your child into a relationship with God.

Many sins that we commit hurt others. Read 1 Corinthians 6:18: *Flee from sexual immorality. All other sins a man commits are outside his body, but he who sins sexually sins against his own body.*

Of course, we also know that immoral sexual alliances do detrimentally affect others as well. Read Ephesians 5:31: *For this reason a man will leave his father and mother and be united to his wife, and the two will become one flesh.* In your own words, define a sexual relationship as God intended it.

1 Corinthians 6:19 says: *Do you not know that your body is a temple of the Holy Spirit, who is in you, whom you have received from God?* The challenge for you as a parent is to pass along a commitment to purity in such a way that your child will take it to heart and determine to live up to it. Here are some ONE THINGS you can do to help your child commit to purity.

- ❏ I will be sexually pure myself. If I'm married, I will be faithful to my spouse. If I'm a single parent, I will not have sexual relations.

- ❏ I will have a zero tolerance policy on the use of alcohol and drugs by my child.

- ❏ As my child grows up, I will be willing to discuss sex with him, always outlining the biblical perspective.

- ❏ I will treat my own body as the temple of the Holy Spirit.

- ❏ I will show my child that fidelity to one person for a lifetime is romantic and worth the wait.

- ❏ I will teach my child about the consequences of sexual immorality and alcohol and drug use.

- ❏ I will monitor TV and movies, music lyrics and class curriculum to ensure that my child does not get an unhealthy dose of an "if-it-feels-good-do-it" philosophy.

❏   I will admit, even to myself, that any child is capable of succumbing to temptation and be an alert parent, especially when it comes to standards of purity for my child.

—————⁓⌒⁓————— **For Your Child Only**

Your child is a unique creation   A vision for your child would not be complete without taking into consideration that your child is a unique creation of God. You may recall from the first session that God created your child for a specific task, according to Ephesians 2:10. What was your child created to do? The potential of your child is unlike the potential of any other. That is a challenge for parents…and an awesome privilege. No one else will possess the opportunity you have to bring out the best in this human being. *Like arrows in the hands of a warrior are sons born in one's youth* (Psalm 127:4).

At first glance, that's a rather curious description of children. But let's put it in context. God often rewarded the great patriarchs of the Bible with children. Having descendants was considered a great blessing. Leaving a mark on this world was often accomplished not solely through one's own accomplishments, but through one's descendants. In just that way, you too will leave a mark on this world. You will accomplish and contribute not just by what you do in your life but – if your child realizes the vision you have for him – your child as well.

Here are some ONE THINGS you can do as you plan to help your child realize his potential.

I will:

❏ get to know my child, becoming an interested – but not obsessive – student of her personality, always trying to understand what makes her tick.

❏ spend time with my child.

❏ give my child the love, support and attention he needs to become an independent adult.

❏ help my child discover and refine her own abilities by offering her opportunities.

❏ let my child take responsible risks, and be ready to catch her if she falls.

❏ demonstrate a love of learning, discussing new ideas and exposing my child to learning activities.

❏ train my child "in the way he should go" by recognizing him as a unique human being with distinctive strengths and gifts, perhaps different from my own or those of his siblings.

Help Me, Help my Child

Hebrews 11 reminds us that many of the great heroes of the Bible did not receive the promises of God in their lifetime. Instead, many realized that it would be their children who ultimately saw the fruit of what God had promised. Not only did these men and women display great trust in God, they loved and valued their children. They were satisfied that if God blessed their children and grandchildren, it was a direct blessing on their lives.

A Plan Comes Together

Review the six key elements that are integral to creating a vision for your child.

1. I want my child to hunger for God and have a relationship with Him that sustains him through life.
2. I want my child to be a loving and contributing member of society.
3. I want my child to make wise choices throughout his lifetime.
4. I want my child to have good friends who will support and love him and help him reach his potential.
5. I want my child to be pure.
6. I want my child to realize his/her potential.

Congratulations! You are on your way toward helping your child develop a full and healthy life. You've written your own instruction book (inspired by God's Word of course) for helping your child become the person God intended – and you, the intentional parent you should be.

Of course, if you manage to conform to every task that you've checked off as desirable in the last few pages, you probably will end up a legend among parents! Instead, you may now be envisioning failure as you resign yourself to the enormity of parenting. There will be days ahead when you fail to live up to those lofty expectations that you've created for yourself as a parent.

There will be days ahead when your child fails to live up to the expectations you have for him, too. Take heart! Chalk it up to experience, resolve to have a better day tomorrow and keep going.

There are concrete ways to take some of the stress out of parenting, but just in case you're really starting to doubt yourself as a parent, be reminded of Philippians 4:13: *I can do everything through him who gives me strength.*

Godly grandparents, friends, counselors and pastors all make good parenting resources, but remember your strength comes from the Lord.

The Daily Dozen For Effective Intentional Parenting

1. I will not do for my child what they can do for themselves – when I do I weaken them.

2. I will not over-react when my child over-reacts; when I do we both lose.

3. I will not rescue my child from their mistakes; if I do I have cheated them from learning.

4. I will not treat my teenager like a child even thought they are acting like one; when I do I create resentment.

5. I will not be dissuaded from doing right, despite anger, tears, cursing or threats; when I do I am an irresponsible parent.

6. I will pick battles carefully because it's more important to be the right parent than to be right.

7. I will give lots of encouragement because it will help my child to build confidence.

8. I will provide training, instruction and support as needed, because that's my job.

9. I will pray daily for my children because my children belong to God.

10. I will use a heart of understanding when my child is hurting, confused, searching and frustrated.

11. I will use a head of caring when my child has questions, needs guidance and wants answers.

12. I will use a hand of logical and natural consequences when my child needs discipline.

About the Author

When it comes to parenting, marriage, and other relationship issues, people are turning to best-selling author, counselor and radio personality Dr. Randy Carlson. Recognized as an advocate for the family, Randy hosts *Intentional Living*, a live daily call-in program syndicated to radio stations nationwide. Randy serves as president of Family Life Communications Incorporated, the parent company of *Intentional Living* and Family Life Radio. Randy has written or coauthored five books and his sixth book, *The Power of One Thing*, released October 2009. Randy is a licensed marriage and family therapist with a doctorate in counseling psychology and has over 27 years of counseling experience.

For more information about Intentional Parenting go to TheIntentionalLife.com

The Parenting Challenge

In this seven week small group study, you'll get simple and easy tools you need to be a successful parent and raise a responsible adult! Whether it's for your Life Group, Bible Study or Sunday School class, you'll learn parenting secrets in this fun, entertaining and informative study from Dr. Randy Carlson.

Session titles include these plus more:
- The Four Laws of Intentional Parenting
- Powering Down and Parenting Up
- Intentional Parents Play All Four Quarters
- **Bonus Session:** Overtime Parenting - Parenting the Adult Child

You can win the parenting challenge!

Love Your Marriage: Lessons on Intentional Marriage

Intentional Living introduces Love Your Marriage: Lessons on Intentional Marriage. In this seven-week study from Dr. Randy Carslon you'll learn practical steps toward building and maintaining a vibrant, intimate and lasting marriage.

Session titles include:
- Understanding your spouse's DNA
- Having somewhere to go together
- Communicating until things get better
- Checking marital vital signs regularly
- Facing marital dips together
- Expectations – Reality = Marital Disappointment
- Giving lots of affection

Small Group Study Leader's Kit Includes:
- Seven teaching sessions on four DVDs
- Audio version of each session on CD
- Leader's Guide
- Participant Workbook*
- Promotional Materials
- ONE THING wristband

* Additional Participant Workbooks are sold separately.